Teen Investing / Personal Finance Terms 101

101 of the Most Important Financial Terms any Investor Should Know

Teen Investing / Personal Finance Terms 101

101 of the Most Important Financial Terms any Investor Should Know

by

Jack Rosenthal

Copyright © 2021 by Jack Rosenthal
All rights reserved. No part of this book may be reproduced, scanned,
or distributed in any printed or electronic form without permission.
First Edition: [March 2021]
Printed in the United States of America
ISBN: [ISBN number with hyphens]

DEDICATION

This book is dedicated to my loving grandfather who helped me set up my first investment account when I was 8 years old and has helped me in business, investing, and life ever since.

Table of Contents

Essential Debt terms 8

Essential Investing terms 10

Stock Market terms..14

Additional terms..16

Government-related terms 21

Types of Investors 24

Investment terms 29

Securities...31

Stock options 34

Personal Finance terms 39

Bonus + ...48

Jack Rosenthal

Legal Disclaimer

The information provided in this book is for informational purposes only and is not intended to be a source of advice or credit analysis with respect to the material presented. The information and/or documents contained in this book do not constitute legal or financial advice and should never be used without first consulting with a financial professional to determine what may be best for your individual needs.

The publisher and the author do not make any guarantee or other promise as to any results that may be obtained from using the content of this book. You should never make any investment decision without first consulting with your own financial advisor and conducting your own research and due diligence. To the maximum extent permitted by law, the publisher and the author disclaim any and all liability in the event any information, commentary, analysis, opinions, advice and/or recommendations contained in this book prove to be inaccurate, incomplete or unreliable, or result in any investment or other losses.

Content contained or made available through this book is not intended to and does not constitute legal advice or investment advice and no attorney-client relationship is formed. The publisher and the author are providing this book and its contents on an "as is" basis. Your use of the information in this book is at your own risk.

My name is Jack Rosenthal. I'm the author of "Teen Investing", one of the top selling books on teenage investing. I've now decided to write a second booklet compiling the top 101 Investment / Personal Finance terms I think any young investor (or investor in general) should know.

Enjoy!

---

1. Revenue

Revenue is by far the most important number when looking at business or financial statements. Revenue is the total sales of a company. If you don't have revenue you don't have a business. Teenagers create new business ideas every day, but only a small fraction will actually earn $1 in revenue. Until you've produced revenue you aren't in business.

2. Profit

Possibly the second most important number when looking at the health of a business. (By the way I promise the terms will get more complex, I just figured it's good to start with the basics). Profit is the amount of money you earn. It is your revenue minus your expenses. Whatever amount you're left over with at the end is your profit. Profit is what you take home at the end of the day. It is effectively your salary for owning a business.

These are probably the TWO most fundamental terms in the business world. I am aware that 90+% of readers purchasing this book are already aware of what they are, but I felt it necessary to include them anyway (simply based on their sheer importance).

Now let's get into all the terms you might not know.

3. COGS

This refers to your cost of goods sold. It is essentially the cost of producing your product. Say for example you ran a computer company and you sold computers to the public. You sell your computers for $1000 and the materials necessary to produce the computer cost $500. If you only sold one computer, your COGS is $500. In addition, your gross profit is $500. Your gross profit is your COGS ($500) subtracted from your revenue ($1000). This leaves $1000-$500 for a total of $500. Lastly your gross profit margin would be 50%. That's your gross profit divided by your revenue. In this case that's $500/$1000.

4. EBIDTA

Possibly the most important term in the modern finance world. EBIDTA is your Earnings Before Interest, Deprecation, Taxes, and Amortization. Your earnings are essentially your profit. However, oftentimes (especially new business owners) don't take into account all the expenses that go into their profits because the money doesn't necessarily leave your bank account. Here's an image I found online to help explain i

INCOME STATEMENT					
			Year ended December 31,		
(in millions)		2017	2016	2015	201.
Revenue		$22,000	$20,000	$15,000	$10,00
COGS		3,200	3,200	3,000	2,50
Gross Profit		18,800	16,800	12,000	7,50
Depreciation	+	500	500	450	40
SG&A		300	300	300	30
Interest	+	50	50	50	5
Earnings Before Tax		17,950	15,950	11,200	6,75
Tax	+	3,590	3,190	2,240	1,35
Net Earnings	+	14,360	12,760	8,960	5,40
EBITDA	=	$18,500	$16,500	$11,700	$7,200

Image source:
https://courses.corporatefinanceinstitute.com/courses/financial-analysis-certificate-course-online

What's great about this income statement is it already covers all the terms we went over plus it includes EBITDA. In this example, your net earnings (profit) are $14,360, but your EBITDA is $18,500. EBITDA will almost always be higher than net income because you are adding back certain expenses which are considered to be non-operating expenses and therefore less representative of the true operating performance of the business.

Now what are Interest, Taxes, Depreciation, and Amortization?

Interest - A fee paid by a borrower to a lender in exchange for a loan. For example, if someone lends your business $1000 for one year, and at the end of the year you agreed to pay them back the original $1000 plus $50. The $50 would be interest.

Taxes - Pretty self-explanatory.

Depreciation - Depreciation is a "a reduction in the value of an asset with the passage of time, due in particular to wear and tear" (Dictionary.com). Here's a simple example to explain depreciation. If your business purchases a donut maker for $500 to produce donuts, and you expect that donut maker will last for 10 years and then break and become completely useless then your business would lose $50 each year in depreciation. $500 (the cost of the product) / 10 years (the amount of years you expect it to last) = $50 (the yearly depreciation).

Amortization – Similar to depreciation, amortization typically refers to the recognition of the annual reduction in the value of either a loan or an intangible asset. Amortization is the amount of principal you pay down on a loan. For example, let's say you purchase a home for $120 and borrow $100 from the bank in order to purchase the home. The terms of the loan are that you'll pay the bank an annual interest rate of 5% in exchange for the loan and you'll pay back 2% of the principal each year. The principal is the $100 original loan amount. Your amortization is the 2% you paydown each year, or $2. On this loan you'd be paying a total of $7/year ($5 in interest and $2 in amortization).

Now (going back to the example) you should have a clearer understanding of the net earnings as well.

The net earnings of a business are the company's "bottom line" net profits.

5. **Appreciation**

The increase in the value of an asset over time.
Suppose you invest $10,000 in a piece of real estate. If two years later that same piece of real estate is now worth $11,000, you gained $1000 in appreciation.

6. Book value

A company's assets minus its liabilities. The value of all the assets you own (such as a building, machinery, etc.) minus the liabilities (such as debt you owe) is the book value.

7. Accounts payable

Money you owe for goods or services that you purchased in the ordinary course of your business. For example, if you purchase boxes for your shoe store for $50 and promise to pay the company that sold you the boxes at the end of the month your business would have $50 in accounts payable.

8. Accounts receivable

Money that is owed to you for goods or services that you sold in the ordinary course of your business. For example, if a customer bought shoes from your store for $100 but promised to pay you at the end of the month, your business would have $100 of accounts receivable.

Essential Debt terms

9. **APR**

    Annual percent rate. This is essentially the same thing as an interest rate.

10. **LTV**

    Loan to Value - This is a percentage representing how much debt you can borrow on an asset. For example, if you are interested in purchasing a home and the bank said they would give you a 75% LTV ratio, that means they would be willing to loan you 75% of the cost of the home. So, if the home cost $100, they would be willing to lend you $75. You would be required to put up the other $25.

11. **Equity**

    This represents the $25 you put into the house in the previous definition. Equity also refers to the net value of a company to its shareholders after paying off all debts. For example, if you buy shares of Facebook in the stock market, you are buying a (very small) share of Facebook's equity, which means you own a tiny percentage of what Facebook is worth after all debts are paid.

12. Debt-to-Income (DTI)

–This ratio represents the debt you owe divided by your income. If you owed $100/month for a mortgage and you had $200/month in income your DTI would be 50%.

13. Collateral

An asset a lender can seize in the event you don't repay a debt. The most common collateral people put up are their houses on a mortgage. If a borrower doesn't pay their mortgage the bank has the right to own their house after a certain period of time passes.

Essential Investing terms

14. Investor

Someone who risks capital seeking a financial gain. If you own a share of stock, you're an investor.

15. Fixed Income Vs. Equity

These are the two core different types of investments. Fixed income is essentially a loan. There are hundreds of variations but essentially one party agrees to pay another party a certain (fixed) rate each year in exchange for capital. Equity is much more of a gamble. An investor puts up capital in exchange for ownership in a company. The investor has no guarantee he will make back all of (or any of) his or her capital. When a bank lends someone money to purchase a home that is a fixed income investment. When an investor purchases a share of stock in a company (like Apple) that's an equity investment. The investor now owns a piece of the company, in this case Apple, Inc.

16. Stock

A piece of ownership in a company. A unit of stock is called a share. Stocks are traded on exchanges called stock exchanges. The two largest are the NYSE (New York Stock Exchange) and the Nasdaq.

17. IPO

Companies initially sell stock to the public through something called an IPO or initial public offering. An initial public offering is the first time shares of a company are traded on a stock exchange, a way in which "the public" can purchase the stock. This is also referred to as when a company goes "public". This term is used because it's the first time the general "public" (me, you, your grandmother etc.) can purchase shares in the company. Prior to this it is much more difficult for the average investor to invest in the company because it would require huge amounts of capital plus access to a seller who was interested in selling a certain amount of their stock. The stock market standardizes all of this information and allows "average" investors to own pieces of enormous companies.

Personal Finance Terms 101

18. Bear Market Vs. Bull Market

This refers to the general direction the stock market has been trending recently. If in the last month or two to one year the stock market has been trending down, the stock market would be referred to as a "bear market". If the opposite has happened and the stock market has been trending up over the last one month to one year the market would be referred to as a "bull market".

Image source:
https://www.pinterest.com/pin/92816442291689097/

19. Bid Vs. Ask Vs. Bid-Ask Spread

The bid price is the highest price a buyer will pay for a security and the ask is the lowest price a seller will sell a security for. A security is an exchange traded asset. A stock, for example, is a security. It's an asset traded on the stock exchange. Let's say a buyer is seeking to purchase a share of Amazon stock and the highest price they are willing to pay is $100 and a seller is willing to sell a share of Amazon stock and the lowest price they are willing to sell it for is $120, the bid-ask spread is $20. That's the difference in price between the highest price a buyer is willing to pay and the lowest price a seller is willing to sell the stock for. If they end up meeting in the middle (and this is all done electronically) at $110 the stock will trade for $110 and the new stock price becomes $110. A stock price is just the most recent price a stock traded for. For the largest companies millions of shares trade each day, and that is what causes the fluctuations in stock prices throughout the day.

Stock Market terms

Here's a screenshot of the yahoo finance portal view of Alphabet Inc., as the parent company of Google.

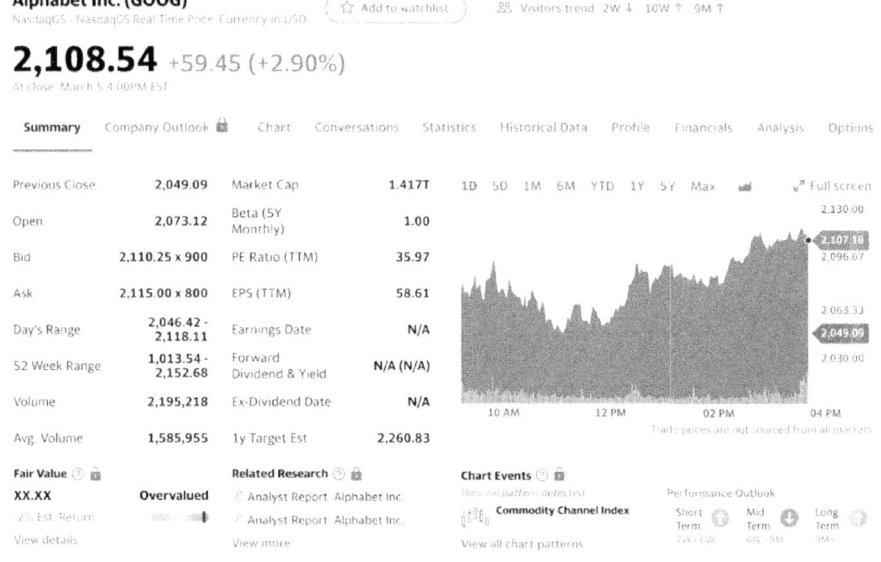

Image source: **Yahoo Finance**

I'll go over the most important terms you need to know.

20. 52-week range

The highest and lowest amounts the shares traded for in the last 52 weeks.

21. Market Cap

The total value (market capitalization) of the company. This is all the shares of the company multiplied by the price of all the shares. For example, if there are 1,000,000,000 shares of Google and the price per share is 2,108.54 the total market cap is $2,108,540,000,000.

22. Dividend

In this case the dividend is N/A or not available. This often means the company doesn't pay a dividend, which in Google's case it doesn't. Oftentimes high growth stocks don't pay dividends because they reinvest all their profits back into the company. A dividend is a sum of money paid regularly (typically quarterly) by a company to its shareholders.

23. P/E Ratio

This is the total market cap of the company divided by the total earnings of the company. In this case Google's net earnings are approximately $39.2 billion. The P/E ratio is $1.41 trillion / $39.2 billion which is approximately 35.97.

24. EPS TTM

The earnings per share in the last 12 months. This takes the total earnings of the company and divides them by all the shares.

Additional terms

Valuation Measures							
	Current	12/31/2020	9/30/2020	6/30/2020	3/31/2020	12/31/2019	
Market Cap (intraday) [5]	1.36T	1.19T	994.60B	964.51B	795.03B	921.14B	
Enterprise Value [3]	1.25T	1.08T	889.66B	864.09B	691.32B	813.71B	
Trailing P/E	34.58	33.88	32.33	28.54	23.65	28.70	
Forward P/E [1]	29.76	30.58	26.39	33.90	21.37	24.51	
PEG Ratio (5 yr expected) [1]	1.44	1.54	1.68	2.89	1.25	1.86	
Price/Sales (ttm)	8.14	7.04	6.13	5.91	5.02	6.03	
Price/Book (mrq)	6.14	5.56	4.80	4.73	3.95	4.72	
Enterprise Value/Revenue [3]	6.85	18.97	19.27	22.56	16.80	17.66	
Enterprise Value/EBITDA [6]	20.21	48.03	52.69	74.01	63.51	57.57	

Financial Highlights

Fiscal Year

Fiscal Year Ends	Dec 31, 2020
Most Recent Quarter (mrq)	Dec 31, 2020

Profitability

Profit Margin	22.06%
Operating Margin (ttm)	22.58%

Management Effectiveness

Return on Assets (ttm)	8.65%

Trading Information

Stock Price History

Beta (5Y Monthly)	1.00
52-Week Change [3]	73.46%
S&P500 52-Week Change [3]	39.88%
52 Week High [3]	2,152.68
52 Week Low [3]	1,013.54
50-Day Moving Average [3]	2,013.84
200-Day Moving Average [3]	1,739.77

Image source: **Yahoo Finance**

25. Enterprise value

The total market cap of a company + debt – cash. Think of this as the "full" value of a business (not just the equity portion).

Financial Highlights		Trading Information	
Fiscal Year		**Stock Price History**	
Fiscal Year Ends	Dec 31, 2020	Beta (5Y Monthly)	1.00
Most Recent Quarter (mrq)	Dec 31, 2020	52-Week Change [3]	73.46%
		S&P500 52-Week Change [3]	39.88%
Profitability		52 Week High [3]	2,152.68
Profit Margin	22.06%	52 Week Low [3]	1,013.54
Operating Margin (ttm)	22.58%	50-Day Moving Average [3]	2,013.84
Management Effectiveness		200-Day Moving Average [3]	1,739.77
Return on Assets (ttm)	8.65%		
Return on Equity (ttm)	19.00%	**Share Statistics**	
		Avg Vol (3 month) [3]	1.59M
Income Statement		Avg Vol (10 day) [3]	1.75M
Revenue (ttm)	182.53B	Shares Outstanding [5]	329.87M
Revenue Per Share (ttm)	268.10	Float	607.3M
Quarterly Revenue Growth (yoy)	23.50%	% Held by Insiders [1]	5.86%
Gross Profit (ttm)	97.8B	% Held by Institutions [1]	68.10%
EBITDA	54.9B	Shares Short (Feb 12, 2021) [4]	2.75M
Net Income Avi to Common (ttm)	40.27B	Short Ratio (Feb 12, 2021) [4]	1.65
Diluted EPS (ttm)	58.61	Short % of Float (Feb 12, 2021) [4]	N/A
Quarterly Earnings Growth (yoy)	42.70%		

Image source: **Yahoo Finance**

26. Profit Margin

The net profits of the company divided by total revenue. This shows how profitable a business is since it states a percentage of every dollar of revenue that ends up as profit. A "low margin" business would have a profit margin of 3-5%, while a "high margin" business (such as Apple or Google) could have a profit margin of 20-30%.

27. Return on Equity

The ROE or Return on Equity is the company's net income divided by the company's shareholder equity. The shareholder

Breakdown	12/31/2020	12/31/2019	12/31/2018	12/31/2017
> Total Assets	319,616,000	275,909,000	232,792,000	197,295,000
> Total Liabilities Net Minority Int...	97,072,000	74,467,000	55,164,000	44,793,000
> Total Equity Gross Minority Inte...	222,544,000	201,442,000	177,628,000	152,502,000
Total Capitalization	236,476,000	205,400,000	181,578,000	156,445,000
Common Stock Equity	222,544,000	201,442,000	177,628,000	152,502,000
Capital Lease Obligations	12,840,000	12,009,000	62,000	26,000
Net Tangible Assets	199,924,000	178,839,000	157,520,000	133,063,000
Working Capital	117,462,000	107,357,000	101,056,000	100,125,000
Invested Capital	236,476,000	205,400,000	181,578,000	156,445,000
Tangible Book Value	199,924,000	178,839,000	157,520,000	133,063,000
Total Debt	26,772,000	15,967,000	4,012,000	3,969,000
Share Issued	675,222	688,335	695,556	694,783
Ordinary Shares Number	675,222	688,335	695,556	694,783

equity of a company is a company's assets minus its debts.

Image source: **Yahoo Finance**

28. Total assets

The total value of all the assets of a company including factories, hardware, machinery, real estate, cash, accounts receivable, investments, etc.

29. Total capitalization

Total assets minus total liabilities. This is the same thing as the company's equity value.

30. Net tangible assets

Total assets of a company minus any intangible assets. Intangible assets are anything you can't "touch" like goodwill (brand value), patents, and trademarks.

31. Tangible book value

The total book value minus any intangible assets.

32. Leverage

The ratio of a company's debt to equity. If a company has $25 of equity and $75 of debt, the company's leverage is 3x.

33. Hedge fund

An investment fund (a way of investing alongside other investors), which uses a variety of methods to seek higher returns while minimizing risks. Hedge funds also may invest with borrowed money in order to realize greater gains.

I thought it would be cool to include a list of the highest paid hedge fund managers in the world. The top 5 highest paid hedge fund managers in 2020 are as follows:

5. **Ken Griffin**
   Hedge Fund: Citadel
   Earnings: $1.8 billion
   Fund Return: 24%

4. **Stephen Mandel**
   Hedge Fund: Lone Pine
   Earnings: $1.8 billion
   Fund Return: 23%

3. **Izzy Englander**
   Hedge Fund: Millennium Management, LLC
   Earnings: $2.2 billion
   Fund Return: 26%

2. **Jim Simons**
   Hedge Fund: Renaissance
   Earnings: $2.6 billion
   Fund Return: 76%

1. **Chase Coleman**
   Hedge Fund: Tiger Global
   Earnings: $3.0 billion
   Fund Return: 48%

Source for this data:
https://markets.businessinsider.com/news/stocks/top-15-highest-earning-hedge-fund-managers-of-2020-2021-2-1030067257

34. Asset Manager

The role of an asset manager is to decide what portion of a client's portfolio to allocate to different types of investments.

Government-related terms

35. 1099

A government tax form one receives if one is self-employed. In other words, if you own a business and are considered self-employed you may receive 1099 tax forms from your clients and pay taxes based on the information on the form.

36. 10-year Treasury Note

10-year Treasury notes are essentially bonds the government issues which will be paid back in full after 10 years. The federal reserve controls the rate on the 10-year Treasury. The higher the 10-year Treasury rate is, the higher the interest rate on a mortgage and all other interest rates on loans issued by banks.

37. Federal Reserve

The Federal Reserve Bank is the central banking system of the United States. It was created in 1913 by the Federal Reserve Act. It was created in order to control the monetary system and in order to prevent financial crises. The Fed controls how much money is in circulation and also sets interest rates.

38. Inflation

A general increase in pricing and fall of the purchasing value of money. Inflation is when the value of a $1 starts to decrease. Here's a perfect example to illustrate it. In 1920 you could buy a house for $10,000, now you can purchase a used car for $10,000. Over time, $1 is worth less and less (it has less "purchasing power"). One factor which causes inflation is when the government (Federal Reserve) prints more money. The more total dollars in the system the less value each dollar is worth.

39. GDP

Gross Domestic Product. The gross domestic product is the total value of all the goods and services products in a country in one year. Here's a list of the GDPs of the 10 largest countries:

Per the International Monetary Fund (2020 estimates)[1]

Rank	Country/Territory	GDP (US$million)
	World[20]	83,844,988
1	United States	20,807,269
2	China[n 2][n 3]	14,860,775
3	Japan	4,910,580
4	Germany	3,780,553
5	United Kingdom	2,638,296
6	India	2,592,583
7	France	2,551,451
8	Italy	1,848,222
9	Canada	1,600,264
10	South Korea	1,586,786

Image source: https://en.wikipedia.org/wiki/List_of_countries_by_GDP_(nominal)

Types of Investors

40. Private Equity

Private equity is equity that is invested in any nonpublic company. Private equity investors purchase a piece of (or all of) the total equity in a private company. Let's say there's a furniture store chain worth $100 million. A private equity investor might purchase 20% of the company for $20 million. The goal of private equity investors is to increase the value of their investment through increasing the value of the company. They can either do this passively and hope the management increases the value of the company and pay consistent dividends on their equity investment, or actively and get personally involved in helping the company grow.

41. Venture Capital

Venture capital is a form of private equity investing; however, it focuses on investing in early-stage high growth companies Some examples of venture capital firms are Sequoia, which was an early investor in Google, and Greylock, which was an early investor in Facebook. Of course, those were wildly successful investments. Many other investments made by venture capital firms end up worthless.

42. Angel Investor

An angel investor is a venture capitalist but is just one individual. Generally, venture capitalists are large institutions and companies. An angel investor is just one individual generally with a high net worth. A great example of a venture capitalist is Mike Markula. He invested $80,000 in exchange for an equity investment in Apple Inc. early on. Before Apple went public he owned **one-third** of the company. Today his net worth is $1.2 billion.

43. ETF

Exchange traded fund. An ETF is a stock that is actually a fund. Unlike a traditional fund which you can only purchase or sell once a day, an ETF is the same thing except you can buy and sell it during market hours.

44. Index fund

An index fund is essentially a collection of several stocks. The purpose of an index fund is to represent the broad market. One of the most commonly known index funds is the S&P 500 which is a collection of the 500 largest companies on the U.S. stock market. Investing in the S&P 500 allows you to invest in all 500 companies without having to individually buy each one.

45. Open end mutual funds

A mutual fund is an investment vehicle which is funded by shareholders and is managed by a manager. Typically, the manager will charge a management fee in order to manage the fund. It is "open" because investors can put money in or take money out at any time.

46. Pension plans /Pension funds

A pension plan is a retirement account set up by a company for its employers. A pension plan typically requires a company/organization to make certain contributions for a pool of funds set aside for the workers' benefit. A pension is typically given to someone when they retire from their employer. The largest pension fund is CALPERS, the California teachers' pension plan.

47. Family offices

Family offices are private wealth management firms which are meant for high-net-worth individuals and families. Typically, families with over $100 million have a family office which invests their money.

48. Endowment fund

Personal Finance Terms 101

An investment fund set up by a foundation. Typically, large universities all have endowments. The largest university

41.9 billion USD
2020

People also search for

 Yale University
31.11 billion USD (2020)

 Stanford University
27.7 billion USD (2019)

 Princeton University
25.9 billion USD (2018)

endowment is Harvard University with an endowment of $41.9 billion. Large charities also typically have endowment funds.

49. Quant fund

A quant fund or quantitative fund is a fund which uses quantitative analysis to make investments. Essentially quant funds use highly complex math equations in order to beat the market. One of the largest quant funds is the Medallion fund run by Renaissance Technology. Amazingly, it has had a compounded return of over 40% after fees from 1988-2018.

50. Investment bank

A financial service company that acts as an intermediary for complex financial transactions. For example, when a company goes public and engages in an IPO, they would hire an investment bank to sell the stock to the public. Typically, investment banks are paid 1-7% of the money they raise.

51. REIT

Real Estate Investment Trust. These are public companies which only purchase, buy and sell real estate. They are required to distribute 90% of their earnings to shareholders which is often why they pay high dividends.

Investment terms

52. IRR - Internal Rate or Return.

This is a complex financial equation but essentially it calculates an investor's rate of return on their money, while also incorporating discounted cash flow analysis. In the modern finance world $1 today is worth more than $1 tomorrow because $1 today can be invested and earn more money. Let's say an investor invested $100 in each of two different investments. In the first investment the investor earns $10 each year for two years and then receives his $100 back. In the second investment the investor receives $0 the first year and $20 the second year and then receives all his money back. The IRR would place a higher value on the first investment because he received more money sooner.

53. NAV - Net Asset Value.

The total assets of a company minus the total liabilities. If a company had $100 in assets and $20 in liabilities the NAV would be $80.

54. Alpha and Beta

Beta is the general market rate of return. For example, for the stock market the beta is considered the S&P 500 which produced an average return of 8.2% from 2000-2020. The beta would be considered 8.2%. For asset managers who invest in a similar market any return they produce above 8.2% would be their "alpha". For example, if an asset manager produced a return of 12%, their alpha would be 3.8%.

Securities

55. Common stock

This is what most people refer to when they refer to purchasing stock in a company. It is the same definition I used for "stock" (#16). In addition, common stock typically has voting rights in large corporate decisions.

56. Preferred stock

Preferred stock is senior to common stock. In other words, investors in preferred stock get paid before the investors in common stock. Preferred stock is generally less volatile (it doesn't fluctuate in price as frequently), and therefore lower risk, but it also typically has a lower return.

57. Treasury stock

When a company buys back its own shares, the shares become treasury shares. These shares have no voting rights and are not entitled to any distributions.

58. Futures contracts

A contract between to two parties to buy or sell a specific commodity or security at a predetermined price at a specified time in the future. These are typically used when large buyers of commodities are purchasing commodities but don't want to be susceptible to price fluctuation. For example, when McDonalds is purchasing beef it will typically purchase futures contracts to avoid unexpected disruptions in supply and/or price.

Image source: **https://logos-world.net/mcdonalds-logo/**

59. Securities

A security is a fungible and tangible financial instrument which holds some type of value. In simplicity, a security is generally something that can be traded. For example, stocks, bonds, options, etc. are all securities.

60. Commodities

A raw material or agriculture product that can be sold. For example, gold, silver, platinum, wheat, cotton, beef, oil, are all commodities.

Image source: https://www.marketwatch.com/story/gold-heads-for-back-to-back-loss-amid-vaccine-hope-us-dollar-strength-2020-09-03

Stock options

61. Stock option

A stock option gives the investor the right but not the obligation to buy or sell a stock at an agreed upon price by an agreed upon time. There are two types of stock options: puts and calls.

62. Put

These options allow the holder to sell an asset at a specific price (the strike price) within a specific time period.

63. Call

These options allow the holder to buy an asset at a specific price (the strike price) within a specific time period.

64. Strike price

The price that the buyer of the option contract can buy (or sell) the underlying security.

65. Expiration date

The end date of the agreed upon price period between the buyer and seller.

66. Premium

Each buyer of an option pays the seller something called a "premium" for the right to buy or sell their stock at an agreed upon price before an agreed upon time.

Here's an example of how they work.

> *Option contracts are usually traded in 100 share increments. For example, to buy call options on the S&P 500 (ticker: IVV) which is currently trading at $320 you would need to pay approximately 0.80% of that amount for the right to hold an option for a one-month period. However, since the contracts are for 100 shares each, you need to buy 100x at a time so that would be a total of $256 ($320*.008*100). So, if you bought one option contract for $256 and the IVV went up 1.25% that month you would double your money. The reason why you can generate such a high return is because of leverage. That 1.25% is compounded by 100x because your option contract gives you the right to the gains on 100 shares So, for 100 shares at $256 which is a total position of $32,000 (of buying power) a 1.25% increase in share price that month would turn your $256 into approximately $512.*

In order to be a covered call option seller, you would need to hold at least 100 shares of one stock. To use the IVV as an example again, your total position would need to be $32,000 (100 shares x $320 per share). By selling the same options contracts I detailed for 0.8% of the total share value in premiums you would be giving up any rights to any increase in value for that month. However, you would be gaining a .8% return on your investment that month. If you did this every month of the year you would earn a 9.6% return, even if the stock market remained flat for the whole year.

*All numbers are approximately correct.

(excerpt from Teen Investing - the Ultimate Guide to Teenage Investing)

67. Bonds

Bonds are debt issued by an entity. There are several different types of bonds including Treasury bonds which are issued by the U.S. government, state and local bonds, also known as municipal bonds (or "munis" for short) issued by individual states or local governments and corporate bonds (issued by companies). One of the advantages to holding most municipal bonds is that you don't pay any federal or state income tax on the income you receive. Bonds are essentially loans.

68. Coupon

The stated annual interest rate paid by the issuer of a bond. Note that this is different than the yield received by the investor because the investor may purchase the bond above or below the original issue price. For example, if the coupon is 5%, but the investor bought the bond at a discount, the actual yield to the investor will be higher than 5%.

69. Yield to maturity

It is the IRR the bondholder will received assuming the bond matures (and is fully paid off).

70. Par value

The stated principal value of each bond. This is the full amount the bondholder will receive if they hold the bond to maturity. If each bond has a par value of $100, the owner will receive $100 when the bond matures (plus the coupons they have been receiving each month, year or quarter).

71. Leverage ratio

The debt of a company compared to the income of that company. This is often seen as "debt/EBITDA", and is a measure of how much debt a company can reasonably support. Typically, you would want to see this number at 6x or less.

72. LIBOR

London interbank offered rate. The rate that banks lend to each other. Traditionally loan yields are stated in terms of LIBOR + x basis points. However, note that LIBOR is being phased out and will be replaced by a similar base rate.

73. Basis points

1/100 of 1%.

74. Junk bond

A bond with a credit rating below investment grade. Credit ratings are determined based on the company's ability to pay back the loan. They range from AAA, AAA-, AA+, AA, AA- etc. to D. Anything below BBB- is not investment grade.

Personal Finance terms

75. Credit score / FICO score

A number that ranges from 350-850 which the bank has determined based on your likelihood to repay a loan. Generally anything over 700 is considered good. Your credit score will affect what interest rate you can borrow money at as well as how much money you can borrow.

76. IRA

Individual Retirement Account (IRA) is a savings account meant for retirement. You don't have to pay taxes on any earnings you receive from your investments. In a Roth IRA the money is not taxed at all after retirement because the money is taxed before it is deposited. If you believe you will be in a higher tax bracket at the age of retirement Roth IRAs make sense.

77. Roth IRA

A special retirement account set up by individual investors, which allows you to not pay taxes on money you take out of the account after the age of 59 1/2. These generally make sense if you think your tax rate will be higher in the future. In addition, the money in your account (if invested) can grow tax free. In other words, you don't pay taxes on the profits you earn from your investments in this type of account. Of course, there are limitations on how much you can put in, and other rules on when you can take money out.

78. 401(k) Plan

An investment account (named after section 401(k) of the Internal Revenue Code) set up by a company or organization on its employees' behalf. The company or organization may match what the employee deposits into the account up to a certain amount. The money in the account is not taxed until it is withdrawn after the age of 59 1/2.

79. Annuity

An annuity is like a bond except it is a fixed income one will receive for the rest of their life.

80. Bankruptcy

When a person's or company's liabilities are greater than its assets.

81. Certificate of Deposit (CD)

A bank account which pays a higher-than-normal interest rate however, you must keep your money in the account for a certain period of time without withdrawing (typically, 12-36 months).

82. Compound interest

It is believed Albert Einstein once said there is no greater force in the world then the power of compound interest. Compound interest is the interest one receives on the interest plus principal of a previous investment. For example, let's say you invest $100 in an investment and earn 5% interest. At the beginning of the second year, you are now earning a return on $105. If you earn at the same rate of 5% this time you will earn $5.25 because you earn 5% on the original $100 plus 5% on the additional $5 that you earned in the first year. The longer period of time you leave money in investments and re-invest it, the greater your compound interest will be.

83. Savings Vs Checking account

A savings account is a bank account where the primary goal is to leave the money in the account in order to receive interest from the bank. A checking account is a bank account where the primary goal is to spend the money on everyday expenses.

84. Insurance

Examples are homeowner's insurance, car insurance and health insurance. Insurance companies issue policies to homeowners, car owners, etc. and collect annual premiums in exchange for providing a guarantee that they will cover the cost if your home is destroyed, or your car is destroyed/stolen. Health insurance companies operate on a similar business model. People pay them premiums and in exchange in the event there are medical problems, the insurance company pays medical bills, hospital bills, etc.

85. Life insurance

Similar concepts to the previous three insurance policies. In exchange for paying yearly premiums, when someone dies the insurance company pays a certain amount of money to the family.

86. Brokerage account

This is an account with a brokerage firm that enables investors to invest in securities. The largest brokerage firms are Fidelity, Charles Schwab, and TD Ameritrade.

87. Line of credit

Similar to a loan, however a line of credit is "on demand" with the bank. Essentially the bank agrees to loan you up to a certain amount of money at any time and you can repay the loan within the agreed upon timeframe.

88. Credit card vs debit card

A credit card is issued by a bank or company and allows you to make purchases (up to a limit) and you must pay a minimum amount at the end of the month. A debit card is a card which allows you to pay with money directly from your bank account.

89. Money market account

These are saving accounts except they pay a slightly higher interest rate. You can still deposit and withdraw funds daily.

90. W-2 form

The form employers file with the IRS (Internal Revenue Service), the branch of the government which collects all the taxes, in order to record the salaries of each of their employees.

91. Refinance

This refers to "re-borrowing" money that you previously borrowed for the purpose of paying back the first loan. Typically, people might refinance their homes if interest rates are lower. Let's say someone originally borrowed $100 at a rate of 4% to purchase their home. Now, however, interest rates are 3% so the same person can go back and refinance (re-borrow) $100 this time at 3%. They can use the $100 to pay off the previous loan, except now they only pay $3 a year in interest instead of $4.

92. Margin

Using borrowed money in order to invest in the stock market. Usually, banks will lend up to 50% of the value of a stock. Be careful, however, if the stock decreases by a certain amount, banks have the right to force you to sell the stock at a loss in order to repay your loan.

93. Registered Investment Advisor

A financial advisor who works with individuals to help select investments.

94. Tax deduction

A tax deduction is an expense a taxpayer can deduct from his or her gross income in order to reduce his or her total tax bill. Let's say you earn $100/year and pay a 10% tax rate on money you earn which would mean you pay $10/year in taxes. If you donate $10 to charity, now you only pay taxes on $90 ($100-$10=$90). $90 * 10% means you only have to pay $9/year in taxes ($1 less than you otherwise would if you hadn't made the donation).

95. Capital gains

This refers to the profit you make from selling an asset for more than you paid. For example, let's say you purchase a stock for $10 and sell it two years later for $25. Your capital gain is $15. Capital gains tax rates are generally lower than standard tax rates.

96. Trust

A separate legal entity that administers an amount of money left by someone to their heirs.

97. Series 7

The test that all Registered Investment Advisors must pass in order to become a Registered Investment Advisor.

98. Ponzi scheme

A fraudulent investment which generally promises higher than average returns. However, the person who created the Ponzi scheme is simply using the money from new "investors" to repay the investments of previous "investors" plus interest.

99. White collar crime

Financially motivated, non-violent crime committed by individuals or companies typically involving fraud.

100. Insider trading

When someone has obtained secret information about a public company (not available to the whole public) and uses it to trade the stock.

101. Owner earnings

I thought this would be a great last term to include. Owner earnings is the method legendary investor (and founder of Berkshire Hathaway) Warren Buffet uses to determine the value of a company. Owner earnings is simply the total cashflow expected to be earned throughout the life a company minus any reinvested profits. The exact calculation as quoted by Warren Buffet is

"These represent

(a) reported earnings plus

(b) depreciation, depletion, amortization, and certain other non-cash charges...less

(c) the average annual amount of capitalized expenditures for plant and equipment, etc. that the business requires to fully maintain its long-term competitive position and its unit volume".

Bonus +

Financial Titans

Warren Buffet – Warren Buffet is the founder of Berkshire Hathaway, a multinational conglomerate which owns companies you may have heard of such as GEICO, Dairy Queen, Duracell, NetJets, Benjamin Moore and Co, Berkshire Hathaway Assurance, Clayton Homes and many more. He is considered by many to be greatest investor of our time with a net worth of $96.5 billion as of March 2021.

Image source: https://www.marketwatch.com/story/quiet-warren-buffett-has-three-ways-to-win-in-this-market-2020-04-02

Carl Icahn – Carl Icahn is one of the most famous American activists. An activist is someone who uses their shares in order to incite change in a public company. He is famous for hostile takeovers; his most famous takeover was of the American airline TWA. In 1985, be bought the company by borrowing money, then sold off all the assets of the company to pay off the debts. Carl Icahn's net worth is $16 billion as of March 2021.

Henry Kravis – Henry Kravis is the founder of KKR, one of the largest private equity firms. He became famous for LBOs (leveraged buyouts) which is how most private equity firms acquire companies. This is where the private equity company borrows money (uses leverage) to purchase a company while putting in some of their own money as well (their equity). One of KKR's largest purchases was RJR Nabisco for $31.4 billion. It was at the time the largest amount ever paid for a company. Henry Kravis's net worth is $7.3 billion as of March 2021.

I hope you found this booklet helpful! If you're interested in learning more about investing and finance directly from me, check out my virtual course. It's normally offered for $297, but for everyone who purchases this book I'm offering it for just $79. Here's the link to sign up - http://bit.ly/TeenInvestingCourse

Lastly, if you enjoyed what you read and you're interested in booking a one-on-one call with me, send me an email at the address below. There are two options:

1) $80 for a 1-hour phone call

2) $50 for a 30-minute phone call

We can cover topics ranging from teen investing, how to set up your portfolio as a teenager, what investments I'm currently looking at, businesses to get involved with as a teen, personal finance, etc. You can also ask me about anything you're curious about. You can reach out to me at jackrose1824@gmail.com to set this up!

Thanks for reading!

Jack

jackrose1824@gmail.com

Printed in Great Britain
by Amazon